# WHITE COLLAR COMBAT

## THE SWEET SCIENCE OF SELLING

## BY DAVE SABEN

This book is dedicated to my loving wife Margy. Without her loving support this would not have been possible. You are truly my inspiration! I love you baby!

Also to my future White Collar Combatants; my incredible son Dylan, my beautiful daughter Ana and my amazing nephew Andre. I love you all dearly!

# TABLE OF CONTENTS

# INTRODUCTION

Are you feeling a little battered, lately?

A little bruised?

Well, it should come as no surprise. After all, professional salespeople are the combat athletes of the white-collar world. The only difference is that they use words and arguments instead of jabs and combination punches.

The result is still the same: in every fight, there is a winner and a loser. Either you're getting the accounts you should and exceeding your projected quotas each month, or you're not. If you've been on the losing ticket once too often this sales season and have been thinking a little too often about throwing in the towel, then you've come to the right place!

# WHITE COLLAR COMBAT

No matter what shape you're currently in, you're here reading a book called *White Collar Combat* because, let's face it, you've been knocked down a time or two and want to quit getting your ass kicked!

Well, as a boxing practitioner, enthusiast, and sales combat veteran, I'm here to tell you that to become a professional sales person you will need to train your mind and body with the same dedication as a professional boxer.

To an uneducated observer, boxing appears to be a brutal, harsh, and unrefined sport. Two people stand on opposite ends of a twenty-by-twenty square. When a bell rings, their tightly coiled bodies collide in a fiery dance of movement and intentional violence.

But, boxing is not what it appears. It is a calculated sport centered on technique, intelligence, skill, desire, and effective aggressiveness. It is the truest of all sports; the one featuring the most moments of pure physical or spiritual truth.

Anyone who tells you that boxing is a battle of fists has never stood in a ring and exchanged blows with a worthy opponent. It is more a test of wills than anything else. In boxing there are no excuses, lies, or cowardice.

Boxers endure physical punishment every day and embrace the pain in order to learn an opponent's weakness as well as hone their own inherent strengths. The person who wins is not necessarily the strongest or the biggest fighter in the ring, but the one who imposes his will on his opponent and executes the best technique.

# LET'S GET IT ON!

Believe it or not, sales shares many similarities with boxing. Observers and the general public often view sales professionals as harsh, brutal, and unrefined. They are to be avoided at all costs, except when completely necessary.

As in boxing, however, the reality of the profession—and the professional salesperson—is quite different from the public perception. A true sales professional endures constant mental punishment and embraces it in order to expose an opponent's weakness.

The winningest boxers train relentlessly to be the very best at their craft. They run, they spar in the gym, they study fight tapes of opponents, they eat for performance, and they condition their minds for victory.

Pro sellers keep themselves in top mental shape as well, perfecting their craft by reading books, taking courses, and learning from seasoned pros and fighting veterans who are always in their corner. In short, sales profession-als are the white-collar "mental gladiators" of our time, exchanging punches for words, nego-tiations for rounds, and bonuses for champion-ship belts.

To truly succeed in sales, you can't just step in the ring and expect to go toe-to-toe with your opponent in a fair fight. Instead, you need to dedicate yourself to the *science of selling* with the same rigor as a professional boxer devotes his or her life to the *science of winning*.

# THE SWEET SCIENCE OF SELLING

What you are holding in your hand is a field guide to the corporate battleground that is the backdrop for the modern sales profession. This small, simple book is designed to transform a sales journeyman (or an apprentice about to branch out on his own) to an elite sales professional who is truly working at his peak performance.

Everything you need to face, conquer, and beat your opponent is in the pages of this book. Whether you're new to the profession or have been around for decades, this book will give you a new mindset and rekindle the fire you once had for selling at the top of your game. You will no longer view what you do as a job, but as a profession.

Make no doubt about it: after reading and embracing the twelve quick "rounds" in this book, you will be prepared to meet any foe, in any marketplace, and on any turf, and come out the victor.

In addition to the development of the skills necessary to be a successful sales professional, this book also serves as a blueprint for a young professional to navigate through the corporate ring and the career paths that open as a result of true professionalism.

If you want to stay in sales and conquer that world, this book will teach you how. If you want to shift paths, step out of the ring, and conquer the world of management, maybe even leadership, the skills you'll learn here will make you a worthy opponent in that world as well.

Throughout our journey into and out of the ring, I will often refer to the "science of selling." If you're the kind of salesperson who works best on his own instinct, all the better. However, there *is* a science to what salespeople do, and understanding it can only help inform and improve your current instincts.

At the end of the day, everyone who chooses this profession needs to treat it with respect and integrity. As a lawyer adheres to a set of guidelines, principles, and values, so does the professional salesperson.

Be proud of this profession and of yourself or find another path.

# ROUND 1:
## "GONNA FLY NOW,"

*Or: Getting in Shape Before Your First Bout*

*"Sales is a tough racket..."*

**~ Alec Baldwin in Glengarry, Glen Ross**

There is no shortage of people who would gladly call themselves "sales" people, with no actual proof to support their claim. They may be in sales, but are they selling? They may have business cards, but are they doing any business?

They call themselves salespeople, but are they...really? Case in point: there are 306,257,936 people in the United States. According the US Census, there are 14.5 million people in the United States in sales or related fields.

To put things in perspective, that's about 21 percent of our population who consider themselves salespeople. Out of these 14.5 million folks, most dabble in sales. By dabbling, they treat the profession as a job instead of a craft. Some treat it more like a hobby than a job.

In short, they are the journeymen of our profession.

So, what's the big friggin' difference?

# JOURNEYMEN VERSUS PROFESSIONALS: ARE YOU FIGHTING OUT OF YOUR WEIGHT CLASS?

A true sales professional puts as much time and effort into his profession as a lawyer, doctor, or accountant. He recognizes that he has a blend of innate, born skill and consummate training to ascend to a higher level of craftsmanship than mere "dabblers" do. She understands that sales isn't about selling a product or a thing or even an idea, but that sales is ultimately about selling herself—and she sees that as the ultimate challenge.

And the journeymen? The journeymen are the car salesmen that won't shut the hell up about "limited time" this and "incentive" that. Instead of listening to your needs as he talks "at" you, pairing you with the perfect vehicle to fit your budget, style or taste, the journeyman just bullies ahead with the intention of wearing you down or winning you over to his way of thinking. She is the garment sales woman who hovers over you like some spooky poltergeist while you attempt to purchase a simple pair of pants.

They are sometimes clumsy, oafish, without tact or taste. They are outdated and shopworn, like bad caricatures of salespeople they saw growing up, or playing out of their old man's ancient sales book. They are, sadly, what most people think of when they hear the word sales-people, and they do craftsmen like you and I a grave disservice by being dabblers instead of doers; brawlers instead of boxers.

However, the professionals—the true professionals—are the politicians that run our country, the entrepreneurs creating brilliant products, the CEOs of major companies, and the real shakers and makers in the US. After all, without sales, there are no jobs. Sales create revenue that results in jobs and financial security for millions and millions of Americans.

And that's no joke.

It's certainly nothing to "dabble" in.

# WHY SALESPEOPLE ARE BETTER THAN LAWYERS

I once had a conversation with a great friend of mine who happens to be an attorney. (For people that know me, they probably are not sure what is more shocking: that I have close friends or that one happens to be an attorney.) In short, my friend believed that anyone can be a salesperson.

I was pretty shocked by his assertion, and the bold confidence with which he made it. In fact, I was so shocked, that this turned in to a fairly heated argument. I asserted that if anyone could be a sales person, than by that logic anyone who can regurgitate information could be an attorney.

When he asked me for proof to explain my theory, I asserted that a true sales professional is more versed in the art of rhetoric than most attorneys are. Even the most skilled trial attorney is not in court everyday arguing, while a sales professional is always arguing. The art of argument is essential to success in persuasion.

My friend's misconception of the profession was based on the assertion that most people have a certain level of salesmanship that they exercise throughout their lives. For example, interviewing for a job is selling yourself to a potential employer.

Likewise, speaking with a member of the opposite sex in hopes of obtaining a relationship or even trying to convince your wife not to drag you to Bed Bath and Beyond for the third straight week in a row to find that perfect window treatment are both examples of selling in one form or another.

The fact is, my friend assumed that just because the common man can talk his wife into eating at a sports bar instead of a four-star restaurant he can also sell a luxury yacht, timeshare, or widget. To which I say, "Hell no!"

And that's why we're here; Round 1 is designed to show you the difference between a journeyman salesperson dabbling in sales and the consummate sales professional, and to help you understand how you can help yourself move up to the next weight class in the science of selling.

# WHOM ARE YOU FIGHTING WITH?

The first question to ask yourself before tackling the challenge of professional selling is, "Are you getting in the ring for the right reasons?" Sadly, too many sales people enter the profession for all of the wrong reasons.

Some enter it because their parents were in it, others have delusions of huge commission checks, and still others think that just because they were an athlete they should be in sales. All of these are false assumptions. You enter sales because you are smart, enjoy arguing, and above all *love to win*.

Let's not sugarcoat it; this isn't politics, and it's no democracy. And, there's nothing wrong with that. Sales is one of the purest professions on the planet, and with good reason. This is about you going toe-to-toe with an adversary and winning. That's sales. No matter what you sell, how often you sell it, or the technique you use, to sell is to win; or you're simply not selling.

In a profession filled with dabblers, clowns and rank amateurs, to truly be successful in sales you need to take your game to the next level and be a *consummate professional*.

Much like a strong man is unprepared to enter the ring with a trained boxer half-his-size, professionalism is not created overnight. You need to be an amateur first, and before you can turn professional, you need to train.

"Train what?" you might ask.

Simple: train your mind and body until you're the ultimate selling/fighting machine. For that, though, you'll need a trainer.

# WHAT MAKES A GREAT TRAINER?

The greatest boxers have had the greatest trainers. Legends like Manny Pacheco had Freddy Roach, Mike Tyson had Gus D'Amato, and Muhammad Ali had Angelo Dundee.

Who will train you in the science of selling?

It would be nice to go it alone, live in a vacuum, and not have to bolster your strengths and face your weaknesses. But, the beauty of training is that it forces you out of your shell, outside the box and into the ring.

To enter sales in any truly meaningful way, you need to first find a trainer and, hopefully, a *great trainer*. Sometimes your trainer will change as your career develops, however, a trainer—make that a great trainer—is essential to your success.

I want to be clear: I am not going to discuss corporate trainers. Corporate trainers will teach you about the company you work for; a sales trainer will develop your craft. Corporate trainers will attempt to teach you about sales; for example, "Ask open-ended questions." This is a rudimentary sales tactic and the vast majority of prospects have been bombarded by sales folks asking open-ended questions, to "questionable" results.

A great trainer is a person who has transitioned out of a direct-sales role and is now more interested in the development of other professionals. However, it could be a professional sales person who feels the need to connect with a new line of people. My best trainer was Dan Schoepf, who showed me a whole new level of sales.

Dan is a trainer *and* a promoter. (I will discuss the need for a promoter in the next chapters). A great trainer is a person who coaches, mentors and assists in your development. A great trainer forces you to focus on your deficiencies rather than just reinforcing your strengths.

So, what should you look for in a Results-Oriented trainer? Look for a trainer who naturally enhances your strengths, but works even harder on your weaknesses. For instance, if you're a big talker, a great trainer will teach you how to listen. If you're strong in negotiation, he'll refine your cold calling.

It's the same in the ring. For instance, if a boxer has a strong right hand, the best trainers will help them develop their left hook. It's not to take away from the boxer's strength, but to give him an additional tool if his strength isn't good enough. A great trainer is a successful professional who is polished and on a higher level than you. Ideally, the trainer should have experience in your industry of choice.

# TIMING IS EVERYTHING

In fighting, as in sales, timing really is everything. We all want it all, and now, but those who rush, often trip and fall. At the same time, those who wait too long often miss the success they might have achieved in their prime.

Don't be in such a hurry to leap into the ring. Many is the fighter who's had the eagerness knocked out of him—literally—by leaping too far, too fast, too soon. Follow these "rounds" in order and don't just learn your craft but perfect it before taking on too much too soon.

Then again, don't wait too long. The goal is not to learn all of this theory and then never road test it in real life. Foolish is the salesperson who waits all his life to use the expertise he's worked so hard to obtain.

Too many dabblers rush in before they've learned their profession, while others wait too long to test their skill. Instead, trust your instincts—and your trainer—to guide you into the ring at just the right time.

# PARTING WORDS ABOUT LEARNING YOUR PROFESSION

Don't be afraid to get a little dirty, to get sweaty, to get knocked down or, for that matter, to get hurt. Don't think you know it all. The best fighters are those who never underestimate their opponent but, instead, are ready for anything. Being ready for anything means coming prepared, each and every time.

To help prepare you for both the next round and a career as the ultimate salesperson, each "round" ends with three things you can do today, this week, and this month.

- **A Jab (something new you can do today)**: Your first jab is easy; *commit*. Today, right now, I want you to commit to being the best salesperson you can be. While it sounds simple, it will require both short- and long-term commitments to your current and future education. So, are you up to the challenge of committing today?

- **A Cross (something new you can do this week)**: Begin compiling a list of potential trainers to assist you on your journey into the ring as a professional, even consummate salesperson. Work the list constantly; adding names, deleting them, rearranging them, sleeping on them, and then starting all over. Keep it somewhere close—in your purse, on your IPad or laptop or even on your dashboard and continually work it. Before the week is out, contact at least one person on your list to begin the process of finding an actual trainer to take you to the next level.

- **An Uppercut (something new you can do this month):** Don't wait for a trainer to begin seeking that next level of craftsmanship in your sales career. This month, seek out learning opportunities wherever they arise. It could be a weekend seminar, a night class in some technology or skill you're lacking, a networking group that meets twice a month, a support group where you might find a mentor, or even in a tech class at the Apple store so you can use every available feature on your brand new iPhone. The key is to use this month—and every month—to begin fine-tuning your craft.

# ROUND 2:
## AMATEUR BOUTS,
*Or: Paying Your Dues*

When it comes to sales, the tendency is usually to bite off more than you can chew from day one. Bigger, faster, better, sooner seems to be the ongoing mantra for newbie and veteran sales folk alike.

Unfortunately, too many potentially dynamic salespeople crash and burn because they get in too deep, too fast and weren't ready for the kind of hardcore negotiations, psychology, and flat-out lightning-level thinking that goes on at the top of the sales ladder.

It's no different than watching a fighter get in the ring knowing he's unprepared, out of shape, and outmatched. Why is he in there? Because he thinks he's ready and, at a certain point, his trainer can only do so much to keep him out. What will happen? He'll get clobbered, that's what!

In boxing, of course, a fighter who gets in the ring before he's ready can receive serious bodily injury and, in some cases, never get in the ring again. In sales, he doesn't have that luxury. Seriously, though, the salesperson who climbs up too fast, too soon, only has himself to blame.

The good news is that unlike fighters, sales-people can live to fight another day if they step in the ring too soon. The bad news is that it takes a lot of doing to get back on the horse once they've been crushed at the negotiating table once too often or spent a whole month without a single sale.

The question is, why risk it when there are so many entry-level sales jobs to help you refine your craft before you ever go toe to toe with another customer again?

# PROCEED WITH CAUTION; EXECUTE WITH EXPERTISE

If you think you're ready for the top, you probably aren't. That's not to say you're not qualified enough, or smart enough or even knowledgeable enough, but that those at the top never, ever underestimate their opponent. Even at the top, they still think they could be outfoxed, outsmarted, and out-negotiated by the next guy—or the next, or the next—and they're often right.

Even the best fighter climbs into the ring uncertain of his own abilities. All the training, regimen, and mental preparation that goes into a fight still gets in line behind the man-made fear that propels him into the unknown. You just never know what your opponent is bringing into the ring. To underestimate him is to undo your own best interests.

Fighting, like sales, requires a healthy sense of confidence as well as an equally healthy sense of self-doubt. Doubt helps you grow because it constantly keeps you on your feet. Can we ever learn enough? I doubt it. The fact is, there is always something more to learn, something else to discover, some experience to have that will make us better and better salesperson.

That's why starting at the bottom, learning the ropes, and duking your way out of the minor league trenches is the best and, in my opinion, the only way to get to the top of the sales profession:

# THE NINE AMATEUR BOUTS—OR ENTRY-LEVEL SALES POSITIONS—ANYONE CAN GET

To begin a successful career in sales, it is first important to find a sales role that will help you develop your craft. I know it can seem counterproductive to becoming the *best salesperson ever*, but in fact, every champion must start somewhere.

In your case, it's going to be very helpful for you to first master the lower level, "amateur" sales professions before tackling the ultimate sales gigs. So, what kind of jobs am I talking about?

The following are nine jobs almost anyone can get, within reason:

1. **Retail sales person:** I don't care who you are, every sales career should start with a stint in retail. When you work in retail, you first begin to understand the power of persuasion as it relates to generating income. While not every retail sales job is involved in commission, every job behind a retail sales counter enables you to work on your pitch, your closing, your people skills, and your negotiating leverage.

2. **Bartender:** While it might seem that bartenders have a captive audience, there are thousands of opportunities every shift to up-sell a customer on a better call brand, a better beer, a different brand of drink, or even a "vacation" drink. Also, every bartender I know gets an invaluable lesson in how to deal with assholes and the public—though they're often one in the same.

3. **Wait Staff:** Talk about selling yourself. Every server knows that great tips aren't

just generated by the food, the ambience or, for that matter, the service—but by outstanding servers! I know servers who make twice as much as "suit and tie" salesmen, and for good reason: even in tights and a tip apron, they've mastered the art of selling themselves!

4. **Commission-only sales work:** When you think commission-only sales work, something like insurance comes to mind. Selling insurance is an awesome way to wrap your head around presenting something few people want to think about in an appetizing, appealing, and actionable way. Just think how effective you'll be selling something you can actually get excited about when you can get jazzed about selling a cancer policy! As I always say about insurance, "It's a great way to start, but no need to stay."

5. **Bank Collections:** Talk about winning over reluctant customers. Collection reps

are highly incentivized to collect money from folks that do not want to pay. If you can garner high success in this entry-level form of sales, your path is paved for bigger and brighter things.

6. **Car rental companies:** So much of sales isn't in how you deal with the customer, but the corporate surroundings, people and politics that exist at your company. When you work in car rentals, you deal with professionals acting not very professional.

7. **Valet drivers:** Try selling yourself in an ill-fitting jacket while out of breath from jogging a quarter-mile on each sales call, and you'll get the slightest taste of how working the valet stand can prepare you for sales in any field.

8. **Fast food:** Better than bartending for learning how to deal with the ignorant, the harried, the frustrated, the unfulfilled, the unhappy and the unsatisfied. As they

say about New York, if you can make it there, you can truly make it anywhere. The best thing about retail and fast food is that you can literally learn sales from the inside out with virtually no experience, qualifications or education – and still succeed.

9. **Customer Service:** So often sales professionals get so bogged down in the corporate double-speak and brochure copy that they forget to focus on what the customer really needs. Few entry-level sales positions allow a salesperson to glimpse the customer's mindset and rationale like working in customer service.

# SPAR BEFORE YOU SELL

Any respectable trainer knows that all the speed bagging, crunches, jump roping, and sparring in the world won't prepare a fighter, even an inherently great boxer, for what it's really like in the ring.

That's why it's so insanely critical to earn your chops in the amateur world of lower-level sales before climbing into the professional ring. The trick is to stop seeing it as a detour and start seeing it as an absolutely critical part of your own personal sales evolution.

There are between seventy and eighty thrown in the average boxing match. As a boxer, I consider each punch thrown, an education. The more punches I throw, the more educated I become in the art of boxing.

Sales is very similar. In the science of selling, every sale is like a punch—an education. The more educated you are in sales through sales, the more experienced you become and the more ready you are to become a consummate salesman at the top of your game. The problem is too many salespeople get into the ring without ever having landed a single punch!

If you think it's all about your resume, that having worked in several bars or fast food joints or restaurants or insurance companies is going to hurt your chances of landing a top sales spot at one of today's leading companies, think again. Every sales manager I know also knows the value of selling in the minor leagues.

Sales is a level playing field. You walk onto it armed only with your life experiences, your work experiences and, of course, your sales experience. Former bouncers, waitresses, retail clerks, teachers, and even stand-up comics have flourished in sales simply because they've been through the ringer in their former day jobs.

It may sound like going backward, I know, but you can't think that way. Every fighter looks forward to every fight. Why? Because it's training, it's forward motion, it's another step—another punch—toward perfection.

Fighters—real fighters—don't care if they're in a dirty gym sparring against a local lowlife or some spotless ring going toe-to-toe against that Russian dude from Rocky 4; it's all boxing, and it's all another lesson on the long road of life.

# PARTING WORDS ABOUT LEARNING YOUR PROFESSION

Don't be afraid to take your knocks in the amateur bouts. None of your time in retail, fast food, or behind a bar is wasted time; it's all good, you're always getting better and, eventually, you'll be well on your way to being the best.

Here are some things you can do today, this week and this month to help make the most of your time in the amateur ranks, and clear the path for success when you finally go pro:

- **A Jab (something new you can do today)**: Check out who's hiring. Match jobs with your personality style. If you honestly can't see yourself working a cash register, stand behind a bar. If you aren't a night owl, get up early and work the breakfast shift at Burger King. Make a fresh start by opening yourself up to the possibilities that a lucrative sales career is waiting for you—at the bottom of the ladder.

- **A Cross (something new you can do this week)**: Apply. If you're serious about sales and want to be the best, do your due diligence and find a place to work in the trenches. Fill out an application, go for an interview, submit your resume, attend a job fair; whatever you do, this week apply for a job in the amateur ranks—proudly.

- **An Uppercut (something new you can do this month)**: Start your new job; start it with relish. Treat it as if you're already at the top, and honing your craft at the gold-standard level. See every customer, every receipt, every up-sell, or shot poured as an opportunity to hone your craft until it's utter perfection.

# ROUND 3:
## GOLDEN GLOVES,

*Or: Learning the Profession by Doing*

It's not enough just to know your profession; you have to learn your profession. And the best way to learn your profession is to get out there and do it. Case in point: a friend of mine recently went back to school to become a teacher. I knew he'd be a good but I knew that whatever she was learning in school, it sure as hell wasn't preparing him to actually interact with clients.

I'd see him during his internship and he'd be all pumped up over his new career; everything was going swimmingly. "Well, yeah, sure," I thought. "That's because the regular teacher's still in the room. Or, even when he's not, his ghost is!"

He got all A's in his college classes, graduated within honors—the works. He got his first teaching assignment at a local elementary school and was so excited. I congratulated him;

then didn't hear from him for a month. When I finally did, he had done a 180-degree turn.

The kids were horrible. They didn't listen. They acted up—and out. He had already sent three to the principal's office. He hadn't taught them anything, yet he spent his entire day disciplining them. And on and on it went. I hated to hear him so upset about something he'd wanted to do for so long, but I couldn't help but think back to those idyllic days in the teaching program and wonder, "Had they really prepared him for anything?"

Everyone has a plan until he gets punched in the face. It's how he reacts to the adversity that separates him as a salesperson.

Sales is, of course, much the same. Your MBA, your training courses, your HR pamphlets, the big notebooks on how to sell, the scripts, the audios, the books, the seminars...it can only do so much. It's all theory—and, frankly, it's all BS—until you close your first deal; then it becomes real.

# MAKING THE THREE ASSESSMENTS

As you learn to sell from the ground up, you will constantly be assessing opportunities to see if they can help you learn even more. That leads us to something I like to call The Three Assessments:

- **Assess Your Space:** Don't waste a day taking up space where you don't belong. Be mercenary about your own future and don't work in a.) jobs that aren't preparing you for that future or b.) for people who don't respect that future. Ask yourself, "Where are you headed? What are you doing now? How do they align?" If you're not being challenged enough, like my teacher friend wasn't, seek out tougher challenges.. Look at the career path that makes the most sense for you based on education, skill, and desire.

- **Assess Your Trainer:** Next up, ask yourself, "Is your trainer doing enough to take you pro?" After all, the only reason you're fighting in the amateur leagues in the first place is to learn, learn, learn your craft by duking it out on the front lines day after day. You need a trainer who knows where you are currently, what potential you have, and how to take you all the way to the top. If you're not feeling challenged enough, you might need to find a new trainer to take you pro. Listen to people and look for expertise if you're in the market for someone new to train you in the science of selling.

- **Assess Your Earning Potential:** Finally, don't just ask what you're making today, but how this job will help you earn more tomorrow. The best fighters test themselves on a daily basis. For them, comfort is the enemy; it makes them fat and lazy. The best salespeople have the same philosophy; they constantly crave a challenge. As you rise in the ranks from the amateur bouts to the pros, you should *always* be earning more—not less. Even if you switch from a salaried position to a commission-only structure, you should be able to thrive, just not survive. Employers often want to overcomplicate your pay scale. Know this: the best compensation plans can fit on a three-by-five note card!

# MAKING MY OWN ASSESSMENT

My sales journey started on the collection floor of a credit card company while I was still in college. Collection jobs are an ideal place to start because they will hire anyone. (Well, *almost* anyone.) This was an inside sales role. My job was to call folks with poor credit and get them to pay on their overdue credit cards. It was a call center with a predictive dialer so I might take fifty calls in a two-hour period.

I was given a sales script and read from it verbatim. Day in. Day out. It was brutal, and I do mean brutal with a capital B. My first two weeks on the floor, I was getting the shit pounded out of me on a daily basis—repeatedly, angrily, handily all day long. No money collected and a shit ton of hang ups.

It was the boxing equivalent of getting my ass handed to me every time I stepped into the ring. I had to get better, fight back, or wind up in a coma! I decided that the only way to get better was to listen to a few of the more successful collectors and learn from them.

So the next day, I went in early and shadowed three of the company's best performers. They each had different styles, methods of delivery and pacing, but they all had something in common: they all went off script. They trusted their gut, followed a line of reasoning, and came to a logical conclusion. One time they might get aggressive; another they might go soft or somewhere in between.

What I realized is the script was shit and I needed to find my own voice. (Or copy my prospects' voice, tone, and inflection.) I began perfecting my craft of asking questions and listening for words that expressed emotion. Once I would hear an emotional word such as "love," "hate," or "belief," I would focus in on that subject and find the opening.

This method is similar to boxing where you stick your jab out until you gauge an opening or a flaw in the opponent's technique. Once the opponent is exposed, you land a power punch. It's not easy to do, but it is very simple. The only problem is a script can't teach you that.

You have to learn it for yourself.

That's what I did, every day. Like a boxer training for the big fight, I was relentless in my approach to the science of selling. My freshman year in college, I worked sixteen hours a week and out collected folks working forty hours. My inside sales game was pretty tight. I left the script in the dust and focused on more powerful, and personal, winning sales techniques. However, to leave it like this would be like a boxer with a great jab that can't move or throw power punches.

I was good, but I needed to get better. I had mastered a few good techniques that could serve me well in the amateur leagues, but needed more—lots more—to perfect my craft and make it in the pros. I needed to transition to the professional ranks

# KNOWING WHEN TO MAKE THE TRANSITION

I built my foundation and then made the transition to an outside sales role in telecommunications. Telecom was a whole new dimension of sales for me; it was like going up in weight class. This was outside sales where it really counted: face to face, without the luxury of hiding behind a phone where I could be or say almost anything.

My first day on the job my sales manager gave me a pitch book and grabbed a map. He said, "These are our products and this is your territory. I will see you back here at five o'clock and expect to see fifty business cards of places you cold called."

I was scared shitless. I remember driving to a strip mall and sitting in my car just staring at the building. I was a nervous wreck. What if someone said no or threw me out of their business? I frantically called my girlfriend at the time (who is now my wife) and confessed my reservations.

Her response was blunt, and about what I'd expect from my sales manager, not my lover: "Stop being such a pussy!" I wasn't sure if she said this because she had grown tired of me overdrawing my checking account every date we went on or if she was sincerely trying to help and figured a little tough love was in order.

Either way, I was vexed. So vexed, in fact, that I jumped out of the car and started banging on doors. After the ninth door and the second "go fuck yourself" response in a row, it started getting easier and actually became kind of fun.

What's more, I learned something about myself doing outside sales that I never would have learned if I'd stayed doing inside sales: I enjoyed a challenge. I could communicate face to face as effectively as I had behind closed doors.

It was more than a transition; it was an epiphany!

I hit seventy-three doors that day, landed one deal, made $600—more than I had ever made before in one day—*and* booked two appointments. By five o'clock I was able to show my sales manager more than fifty business cards and all the progress I'd made.

If it was an initiation, I'd passed it. If it was an addiction, I was addicted. I came back the next day, and for several years after that. And, after three years of banging on doors, you learn about people and that they are not all that different.

Their responses might be the same, their attitudes and masks might be the same, but at the end of the day, they all want to be sold. You just have to figure out how to do it in your own personal style. As for me, I learned how to be effectively aggressive.

# MASTERING THE ART OF EFFECTIVE AGGRESSION

The key to any boxer's or, for that matter, any salesperson's success is to be what is known as *effectively aggressive*. Very few people respond to flat aggression, which is straight up talking, talking, talking with no interaction. And aggressively at that.

Effective aggression is the art of counter punching. Talking and listening; listening and talking. Telling people something personal about yourself so they open up, just enough for you to see the hole you need to drive straight through. You see the hole and then hit it, just like when you discover a boxer's weakness and exploit it.

Effective aggression is being persistent about what you want in an effective way. You determine what's going to be effective, why it's going to be effective with this particular client and, ultimately, how effective it's going to be.

# PARTING WORDS ABOUT GOLDEN GLOVES

Regardless of your own personal selling style, you'll never know until you learn while you earn. It's important not to see your amateur bouts and golden-glove status as anything less than a solid investment in your ultimate success; everyone has to start somewhere.

I recommend the bottom because that's where real learning happens. There is nothing like…

- An irate customer

- A line of fifteen hungry, breakfast-sand-wich cravers

- A desperate housewife

- A scammer

- An unemployed worker overdue on his bills

- A dick of a boss

- A greedy sales manager

…to teach you what human nature is all about. That's why I say, whatever—fast food, retail, insurance, cold calling, inside sales, collections, take your pick—it's all making you a student of human nature, and that's never a waste of time.

Here are some things you can do today, this week and this month to help make the most of your time in the amateur ranks, and clear the path for success when you finally go pro:

- **A Jab (something new you can do today)**: *Challenge yourself.* Right now, today, get out of your comfort zone. If you only have to make fifteen sales calls today, force yourself to make twenty-five. If you only have to bring back fifty business cards, bring back seventy-five. Whatever it is you're doing today, double or triple the stakes to prove to yourself that you're ready to go pro.

- **A Cross (something new you can do this week)**: *Gain ground.* Keep moving. Start again. Start over. Start anew. Take the next seven days and commit to reinvigorating whatever is working for you. Also, use the time to weed out what isn't. When I threw out that tired, old sales script, my true sales training began. Are you still reading from a script? Throw it out, and start fresh.

- **An Uppercut (something new you can do this month)**: *Transition.* Use this month to assess where you are and begin transitioning to the next level. If you're overachieving in inside sales, transition to outside. If you're used to taking sales calls, transition to cold calling. Mastering one aspect of sales isn't the pinnacle of success; only a sign you're ready to transition into another aspect of sales so you can master that.

# ROUND 4:
## FINDING A PROMOTER,
*Or: The Importance of Allies*

At the end of the day, boxing is all about self-reliance. It's about two men in a ring, and everyone else out. The fighter truly does stand alone, regardless of how many years he's fought, how many trainers he's had, or other folks who are in his corner. In sales, as in boxing, you must be able to stand alone and take the punches, day in, day out—and give them back as well.

No amount of coaching, mentoring, training, blood, sweat, or tears can replace the actions *you* take of your own accord as you trade punches with the very best. Coaches can coach, mentors can mentor, and trainers can train, but they can't take the punches for you. When the bell rings, it's you walking into the center of the ring, not them.

But…but…no boxer truly stands alone when you take into account the years of advice, counsel, and good, old-fashioned horse sense that goes into his development.

We are not islands unto ourselves until we step in that ring; everything we learn outside of the sales process contributes to that very process, and without active promoters we are often unprepared to sell in the first place.

This round is about finding a promoter, and how that will help you stand on your own two feet when the time comes to strive for that champion belt and became an ace in the science of selling.

# WHAT A PROMOTER IS AND ISN'T

First, let's talk about what a promoter is and isn't:

- **A promoter is**: Someone who helps you sell.

- **A promoter isn't**: Someone who sells for you.

- **A promoter is**: Someone you can count on.

- **A promoter isn't**: Someone you can use.

- **A promoter is**: An ally.

- **A Promoter ISN'T**: A mentor.

- **A promoter is**: A proven professional who lets his experience speak for itself.

- **A promoter isn't**: A loudmouth poser.

- **A promoter is**: Your ticket to sales success.

- **A promoter isn't**: A guarantee of sales success.

# THE FOUR TRAITS OF A POWERFUL PROMOTER

Now that we've uncovered what a promoter is and isn't, let's examine what a powerful promoter can do for you:

- **The First Trait of a Powerful Promoter is** *Confidence*: No one can promote you who can't promote himself. Look for a promoter with confidence; someone who is already a superstar in whatever he does. (And remember, it doesn't have to be sales.)

- **The Second Trait of a Powerful Promoter is *Empathy*:** A powerful promoter understands what it's like to be in your shoes. He wants you to succeed, understands what it will take, but is also sensitive to your specific needs and learning styles. That doesn't mean your promoter should be a pushover; only that you want someone you can work with and feel comfortable with.

- **The Third Trait of a Powerful Promoter is *Credibility*:** What has your promoter done? Are you proud of his accomplishments? Is he? A promoter must have powerful past proven performance to help guide you where you need to go in a credible manner.

- **The Fourth Trait of a Powerful Promoter is**
  *Trust***:** No matter how confident he, how
  empathetic, or how credible, if you can't
  trust your promoter, he simply won't be
  any good for you.

# ALLIANCES VERSUS MENTORS

A promoter is not necessarily a mentor,
though he may do a lot of mentoring in his role
as promoter. What you're really looking for is an
ally; someone who can work with you to help
you acquire the traits, experience, expertise,
and connections you'll need to succeed in the
science of selling.

Some promoters are highly connected and
can help give you a leg-up with a job, a con-
nection, a boss, or another promoter. Others
are simply there to figuratively "promote" you;
in other words, to help build up your confidence, your expertise, your abilities, and your
self-worth.

WHITE COLLAR COMBAT

The best promoters do a little bit of both. For instance, Anna recently started looking for a powerful promoter to help her take her sales career to the next level. She'd been doing the marketing for the family business, helping to promote a small string of beach-themed restaurants in South Florida, but was champing at the bit to get more aggressively into the science of selling for a Fortune 500, or even a Fortune 5,000 company.

A friend of a friend introduced her to Jason, a guy who'd been in pharmaceutical sales for the last decade. Jason was no motivational speaker, bestselling author, nor millionaire, but he was a powerful promoter. He lived, breathed, and existed for sales. He read books about sales, took seminars about sales, all his friends were salespeople, and all his vacations were sales retreats with other salespeople.

What's more, he was young, energetic and motivated to help others sell. Jason and Anna began meeting casually at a local coffee shop once a week. There was nothing formal about the relationship, just a solid hour of one-on-one where Anna could ask anything she wanted/ needed to of Jason, and Jason could answer at will and at his leisure.

Jason was an avalanche of information but, also, encouragement. Rather than tell Anna what to do, he would show her. For instance, one day he took a look at the marketing work she'd been doing for the family business and gently suggested she do this, that, and a few more things to generate leads.

The next day, she updated her blog and started working on his homework. Jason and Anna even went to a few local seminars together, and Jason got Anna to join a sales club close to her work that she began going to without him. Gradually, Anna weaned off her weekly meetings with Jason and transitioned to monthly get togethers for lunch or for a walk in the park or along the beach.

They were both busy and the change suited them both. More importantly, promoters are temporary; they come and go—like bosses, like lovers, like mentors. We need them when we need them, maybe we'll always need them, but when we need them the least is when we're ready to branch out on our own and enter the professional world of sales.

Jason helped Anna set up a few interviews with some great companies, prepped her on how to handle them and then...let her at it. Weeks later she was on the sales floor of a booming South Florida furniture store and slowly, but surely, getting her sales legs under her.

That's central to the promoter relationship; you're not necessarily looking for an "in" to promote you in his or her company, but someone to give you the tools you need to succeed in *any* company.

# FIND SOMEONE YOU CAN FEED OFF OF

In boxing, a promoter is always on the lookout for a great new opportunity for his fighters. He's also a kind of surrogate parent, trainer, coach, mentor, buddy, pal, and guidance counselor all in one.

In sales, powerful promoters are proven professionals with a giving heart, a loose tongue, and a patient ear. Like Jason, or even Anna, you need someone relatable, someone sociable, someone you can feed off.

It's not about using a promoter or standing on his shoulders, but learning from him, absorbing his knowledge, skills, and confidence so that you, too, can succeed in the science of selling.

At its heart, working with a promoter is a relationship more than anything else. Get it straight: this isn't networking. You want to network, network. You want a promoter, be invested in giving as much as you're taking.

When it comes to finding a amazing promoter, you're less interested in whom he can introduce you to and more interested in building a relationship with someone who knows how to help you succeed on your terms.

# DON'T JUST FIND A PROMOTER, FIND THE RIGHT PROMOTER: FIVE TIPS TO HELP

The promoter that works for your coworker, your brother, your sister, your neighbor, or your best friend might not necessarily be the right promoter for you. Some people respond to tough love in a way that elevates them, while others feel torn down and end up worse than better. Some people want a coach, others a friend, still others a wise and sage advocate.

The key is to find the promoter that's right for you. Here are five tips to help you do just that:

1. **Timing is everything.** Just as I suggest you spend a few months working in the

amateur ranks of entry-level sales to get your feet wet, take your time finding a promoter as well.

2. **You're in the driver's seat.** When it comes to choosing a promoter, you're in the driver's seat. You don't have to go with your friend's promoter, some motivational speaker, or even the top salesman of the year. Remember that you want someone you can relate to and who can help you. When you find that match, you've found the right promoter for you.

3. **Don't wait for them.** Whatever you do, don't sit around waiting for a promoter to find you. Be active about it; make it a priority.

4. **Let people know.** Don't keep your search for a promoter secret. Send it out into the world and see what you get back!

5. **Go where promoters go.** Go to sales clubs, look at work, look outside work,

talk to people at seminars, and join organizations where powerful people go to meet, gather, and share. Take pride in what you do and look for someone who takes pride in what they do; you can be twice as powerful together.

# PARTING WORDS ABOUT FINDING A PROMOTER

Finding a promoter is a personal journey that begins with action, not inaction. Here are some things you can do today, this week, and this month to help you find just the right promoter at just the right time to take your sales game to the next level:

- **A Jab (something new you can do today)**: *Commit.* Today I want you to commit to getting a promoter. Consider it your first sales job; finding someone who can take you someplace you've never gone before by showing you what's inside of

yourself. It requires the proper commitment to find the right promoter for you,
and you can't start looking until you first
make the commitment to take this next
critical step.

- **A Cross (something new you can do this week)**: *Cooperate.* Start seeking out promoters you think might be a proper fit
for you and begin meeting with them.
Commitment is fine, but you have to
take the next step. This week I want you
to schedule *at least* three appointments
with various promoter prospects.

- **An Uppercut (something new you can do this month)**: *Collaborate.* I don't want
you to rush, but I don't want you to sit on
the sidelines of this great opportunity for-
ever, either. So this month I want you to
actively begin working with a promoter.
And I want you to keep meeting with him
next month, and the month after, as well!

# ROUND 5:
## TURNING PRO,
*Or: Fine-tuning Your
Professional Career*

The difference between a fighter and a professional boxer is that while the fighter might be just as good, train just as many hours, and be just as ready, the professional boxer *makes his living from his fists*.

There is a huge difference between sparring and training, even winning a few bouts, and making the leap to "turning pro." What's more, this is the path the pro has chosen; he has thrown his hat into the ring, so to speak, and said, "I am going to be a professional boxer."

No more part-time jobs in the local gym, no more bartending at night, no more distractions; that's what it takes to fight professionally—complete and utter commitment to the sport.

Obviously, sales is no different. While working in fast food or retail or other "amateur ranks" can obviously help prepare you for irate customers, closing a deal, and time management, you won't fully commit to the science of selling until you're ready to go pro.

This chapter is about that transition phase; that in between time between the amateur ranks and you making the full-time commitment to enter the ring and go toe to toe with some of the best.

Where will you find the confidence you need to make the decision?

How will you budget your time, energy, and even money to make the transition?

Where will you start?

These are the questions we'll be answering in Round 5:

# CONFIDENCE: THE SECRET TO GOING PRO

**Question:** When will you know if it's the right time to go pro?

**Answer:** When it doesn't scare you anymore.

This may be oversimplifying matters a tad, but the fact is that *fear is one of the biggest obstacles to success*. Fear of not being good enough, or smart enough; fear of not being a good enough negotiator, or a good enough salesperson.

Dogs aren't the only ones who can smell fear; so can your competitors, your clients, your customers, your coworkers—even your boss. Be fearful enough and you won't even get an interview, let alone a sales job.

Fear makes us second-guess ourselves, and one thing a good fighter—and a good salesperson—needs is to be absolutely fear-less; in or out of the ring. You simply can't beat your opponent if you can't get over your own fear, insecurities, anxieties, and self-doubt.

There are too many things your mind needs to be focusing on during the sales process than fear. When it comes to the science of selling, the only way to reduce fear, let alone eliminate it, is to replace it with one thing: *confidence*.

One way to combat fear is through knowledge; know yourself, know your job, know your customers, know your skill set(s), know your weaknesses, and by all means *know your strengths*.

Self-knowledge is the first step to self-confidence. One of the many reasons to toil in the amateur leagues so long, in boxing as in sales, is to build up your confidence. It's not a luxury; it's absolutely critical that you not only know yourself, but have self-confidence.

# MAKING THE TRANSITION: THOUGHTS ON TIME, ENERGY, & MONEY

In all careers, there are learning curves. You have to walk before you can run, and you have to run before you can sprint. No time is wasted, even if you've spent the last five years flipping burgers because if you're going to be successful at selling, you're going to have to learn the importance of details.

People skills, handling pressure, management, leadership, politics, bureaucracy, negotiations, thinking fast, thinking faster—these are all skills you can learn in any sales job, no matter how entry-level.

So, why toil in the amateur ranks? To learn, learn, and then learn some more. Still, what are you learning for if it's not to go to the next level? When is the right time to transition from the amateur leagues and go pro? Tackling the three major issues of time, energy, and money will stand you in good stead when it's finally time to go toe-to-toe with the pros:

- **Time:** *Budget your time wisely.* Don't waste it. There is a lot of opportunity in sales to set your own schedule, be out of the office for long chunks of time, or be a self-starter. Some use that as an excuse to slack off, take long lunches, or break out early. Don't be one of them;

use your time to make more time. More leads, more calls, more connections, more closings. If you're going to go pro, be prepared to go pro every day. That requires a time commitment as much as it does a personal commitment.

- **Energy:** *Focus on what matters most.* Energy is a commodity; you can't just sleepwalk through a tough negotiation or you're going to get your ass handed to you on a silver platter. The best sales-people are energetic because they love selling and get pumped about it. It's not an artificial high or energy drink thing; it's internal—the adrenaline pump that comes from facing a challenge and coming out the victor.

- **Money:** *Be prepared to get ahead.* One of the biggest factors in turning pro is transitioning from a regular, hourly, nine to five, clock-in paycheck and relying strictly on your sales skills and commission earnings to pay the rent. It can be a significant challenge if you've been in the amateur ranks so long that the thought of being without a "regular paycheck" is still pretty scary. The fact is, even the best salespeople go through fat times and lean times. Budget for the transition. Set some money aside if you can, or learn to live more cheaply if you must. Don't create a scenario where you can't go pro because the thought of going a week or two without earning a dime prevents you from leaving your day job.

# YOU'VE ALREADY STARTED: MOVING IN THE RIGHT DIRECTION

Going pro is a mindset as much as an income bracket; you won't earn like a pro until you feel like a pro. That's why confidence is so critical to this stage of your career; if you're not ready in the confidence department, you'll fall short in the earnings department.

The key is to have a goal and stick to it. If you're itching to go pro, the timing is probably right—or getting there. Pick a date and focus your energy there. If it's Valentine's Day and it's getting really hard to stomach your retail job, say to yourself, "By July fourth I am going to commit to finding a full-time sales job." If it's July 4, give yourself until after the holidays and start full time job in the New Year.

The good thing about sales is that there are always jobs available. Why? Because many folks try to go pro too soon, leaving open positions when they crash and burn two weeks—or two days—on the job.

Don't rush success. Certainly, if a sales opportunity that's too good to pass up lands on your doorstep, take it! But in the meantime, give yourself the time to become absolutely proficient in your sales skills before making that leap into the pro ranks.

# PARTING WORDS ABOUT GOING PRO: TRAINING CAMP

Going pro is a mindset; it's also a process. There are things you can do every day, every week, and every month to better prepare yourself for the transition from the amateur ranks to the pros; here are three of them:

- **A Jab (something new you can do today)**: *Set a schedule.* Pick a date for your transition into the pros and stick to it. Give yourself time to build up your self-confidence, sure, but if you have no "exit strategy" for the amateur ranks, that's where you'll stay permanently. So, for today, grab a calendar, circle a date, and spend all your time working toward that ultimate goal.

- **A Cross (something new you can do this week)**: *Boost your confidence.* Take stock of what you do well; focus on that. Not every salesperson will do everything well; some aren't good with the details but can talk anyone into anything. Which is more important: the close or the paperwork before and after the close? Both, of course, but you have to know what works best for you in order to be your best. Spend this week focusing on what you're good at instead of what you'll never be good at.

- **An Uppercut (something new you can do this month):** *Make the Transition.* The next thirty days can be a productive transition period for you—*if* you let them. Make connections, make plans, make appointments, make good impressions— and make a move!

# ROUND 6:
## CHANGE WEIGHT CLASSES OFTEN,
*Or: The Gift of Flexibility*

If you've ever known a boxer, you'll know that his diet is *very important to him*. That's because for a fighter, changing weight classes can give him a competitive advantage.

Being at the top of a weight class (at his heaviest weight possible and still be able to fight) gives the heavier boxer an advantage over a lighter fighter who is at the bottom of his weight class.

As much as five or ten pounds can be a critical tactical advantage for a boxer, so if Alec the Assassin is fighting at 160 pounds and Markov the Murderer is fighting at 145 pounds, both may be fighting in the 165 to 140 weight class, but Alec has a decided advantage over Markov because of that extra fifteen pounds.

Likewise, if Markov were to lose just six pounds and move down to the 125- to 139-pound weight class, he'd have an advantage over a much lighter fighter weighing in at just over the limit, at 127 pounds.

So a strong boxer who can lose five pounds to fight in a lower weight class is going to be at an advantage versus that same boxer staying in his weight class where he's much smaller than his opponent.

This constant struggle to fight in and out of weight classes keeps boxers on their toes, continually looking for ways to add muscle and shed fight, while always keeping an eye on who is fighting in any weight class at any one time.

Sales has a weight class, too. There are inside jobs and outside jobs. There is business to customer selling (B2C), business to business selling (B2B), and everything in between. There are industries that are faster-paced and cutthroat, and those that are more suited to a genteel, deliberate sales process.

Which company is right for you? Where will you fit best? Where will you be the most financially and professionally rewarded? Rarely is your first sales job a perfect fit.

Often it takes several jobs, income levels, bosses, and even companies before you're at just the right experience level to deliver just the right amount of service for just the right clientele at just the right company.

How will you know how good you can be—or how high you can go—if you stay put and stick with the first sales job you ever get? Round 6 is about switching weight classes; aggressively, deliberately…and often!

In sales terms, it's about always searching for the right combination of preparation, opportunity, experience, and leadership that is going to help you understand what I call "the science of selling" and prepare you for that next level of going pro.

# KNOW WHEN IT'S TIME TO GO

Here's a simple piece of advice on why it's important to switch weight classes often: *Do not stay at a job with no advancement*. This isn't a volunteer position and you're not doing missionary work; you are here to learn, succeed, grow, accomplish, and earn. And there's nothing wrong with that.

You can do your best, be your best, and perform your best at every company, but it's not always going to be for the same company. Companies have learning curves; they also have glass ceilings.

If you're constantly finding yourself at the top of your department, with a plaque full of awards but a head full of ideas and nowhere to implement them, you might be a big fish in a small pond. It's time to get a bigger bowl!

I'm not talking about becoming one of those leap-frogging sales geeks whose resume looks like a laundry list of two to three week sales job for every furniture store and insurance company within a thirty-mile radius.

This isn't about being flaky or whimsical or irresponsible to those companies that do hire you; it's simply about recognizing opportunities and knowing that they have an expiration date.

It's nice being at the top; it really is. But the top sales person at Company A is often the lowest sales person at Company B. That doesn't necessarily make either salesperson, or company, "better" than the other; it just means that you may have more to learn at Company B.

So, why aren't you applying there? If your ultimate goal is to be a champion-class salesperson, then you must think, train, and act like a champion. One thing champions don't do, in or out of the ring, is rest on their laurels and get comfortable.

Comfortable is for couches; not salespeople. Always try to stretch, learn, and grow in your career. Yes, it's awesome to have a wall full of plaques and your face on the "Salesperson of the Quarter" board every quarter, but recognize that if you're at capacity at one company, there is often something more challenging at another company.

Maybe that will be a bigger company, or a boutique company, or a startup company. Perhaps it will be in a bigger town, going up against tougher negotiators in a higher tax bracket. Maybe it will be in another industry, or working for a guy who literally wrote the book on selling.

You probably already know what I'm talking about. We've all been there; you're ready to move on but not quite ready, either. You just need a little shove; well, here it is: *Do not stay at a job with no advancement.*

If you're at the top, suck it up and go somewhere that will make you work to get back to the top again; and again, and again. Sales is like the unnecessary directions on the back of a shampoo bottle: lather, rinse, repeat.

It can often take months, even years, to learn all a company, position, mentor, or boss has to teach you, but you'll know it when it's happened. And that's when it's time to move on and switch to the next weight class.

# KNOW WHEN IT'S TIME TO STAY

Changing weight classes doesn't always have to be about moving on to greener pastures. You can excel in the same company if you simply commit to upping your game and sucking the life out of every sales experience and opportunity.

Here's what changing weight classes might mean in your current organization:

- **Getting a promotion**

- **Switching to a new product line**

- **Transferring to another position**

- **Increasing your own personal, internal sales quota by X percent**

- **Working with a new partner on sales calls**

- **Taking on more responsibility**

- **Moving to a different sales region**

When you look at it like that, there are literally dozens of opportunities for you to go up or down in any weight class, in any organization. The key is to always be ready to move at a moment's notice, and to not get too comfortable in any one position.

# RECOGNIZE THE CHAIN OF COMMAND

Where can you go from where you are?

Are you at the top already?

At the bottom?

Do you have to move into another department, even another company, to be promoted
or enter into the leadership side of things?

Let's face it: there are a lot of stupid companies out there. A lot! They know nothing about
encouraging people, making employees feel
useful and committed, or even encouraging
them to work harder.

In sales departments, particularly, most
leaders think only of the bottom line: numbers, sales, customers, quarterly reports, up or
down—period. To succeed, you have to know
where you fit on the food chain and quickly
determine where your time is going to be the
most valuable.

Let's be real: none of us is here to win the
Nobel Peace Prize. We're here to sell, grow,
learn, succeed, achieve, make money, and
go far. You don't step into the ring unless you
want to win, right?

So why get into sales if you don't want to be the best?

The fact is, you can sell as well at the bottom as you can at the top. And there are higher and higher levels of competitive selling that will blow your mind if you only give yourself a chance to live, learn, and see what they're all about. Imagine selling your company's wireless plan, widget, or whatnot to... Bill Gates.

Imagine winning a billion-dollar contract to supply the White House with whatever it is you're selling. Imagine taking a meeting with Bill Gates or Oprah about using your company's products. Picture sitting across from the suits at Universal Studios to put their latest superhero on your cups, T-shirts, or visors.

It happens; every day. And by lesser salespeople than you and me, trust me!

The fact is, as sales departments go, so do companies. Your company, like every company, will have a chain of command. In order to achieve your ultimate sales goals, you have to determine where you fit along that chain.

Are you at, or near, the top? What *is* the top? Is it sales manager, team leader, regional VP or, ultimately, CEO? What, realistically, are your chances of snagging the top job? Along what timeline? And is that even something you want?

At some point, most salespeople are eager to get out of the day-to-day sales game and lead, teach, share, and impart their lifetime of experience. Are you there yet? Will you have the opportunity to lead if and when you're ready to do so?

If it's going to be another ten to twenty years before you even get a crack at a management role, let alone a corner office, are you willing to wait that long? Sure, if it's Microsoft, Disney, or Facebook but...what about anywhere else?

You have to take into account your needs with what the company is offering and measure the difference. It's okay to work hard, do a job, look up after a few months/years, and ask yourself, "What's in it for me?"

Look, the company wants what it wants; you want what you want. As long as that's working out for you both, it's a good fit. Whenever it gets too one-sided, you have to be realistic and survey the landscape and decide whether it's time to stay or leave.

# BE F.L.U.I.D. – GO FAR!

The beauty of sales is that once you've learned to sell, you really can go anywhere. Yes, you will always be learning, always be failing, always be succeeding, always be understanding, but even the most basic understanding of "the science of selling" allows you to sell most things at most levels.

To IBM, Target, Apple, Oprah, or Universal? Maybe not yet, but soon. They say in sales to "always be closing." But I think the real key to understanding the ongoing science of selling is to always be moving.

So when you're changing weight classes, you're saying, "I'm ready for the next product, the next mentor, the next manager, the next leader, the next experience, the next skill set… the next opportunity.

In order to move at a moment's notice, you must be F.L.U.I.D. In other words, you must be:

- **Fast:** Good fighters are fast fighters. They are always on the lookout for an opportunity to land a punch, to get another fight, to learn something new. The first secret to switching weight classes often is to recognize, quickly and accurately, where you need to go; and then go there.

- **Light:** Always travel light. Don't turn your cubicle, office, or desk into a second home. Keep what you need on you at all times; in your laptop, your PDA, your iPhone or Blackberry. Be able to walk away from any job, at any time, and onto a new—and better—experience.

- **Understanding:** Don't just watch what happens in sales meetings, conference calls, negotiations, and closings; understand it. If you don't truly *understand* the science of selling, you may sell, but you'll never know why—or how to get any better. Don't sleepwalk through a single day; make it all about learning, getting better, and going places.

- **Intelligent:** Be smart and, if you don't feel naturally smart, get smart. Say what you want about boxers, but the best ones have an intelligence that goes beyond master's degrees and book learning; they have a quick wit and an innate intelligence about what they are doing. Hold yourself to a higher standard of intelligence and you *will* rise to the occasion!

- **Dedicated:** Again, please don't take my advice to switch weight classes often as a suggestion that you should dick people over or leave your colleagues holding the bag. Traveling light and recognizing opportunity doesn't mean burning bridges and not being respectful of those in your rearview mirror. Be dedicated to every job, as long as you're there. Do good work for everyone, at all times, and those who matter will understand when it's time for you to move on.

# SIX WAYS TO CONSISTENTLY CHALLENGE YOURSELF

Consistently challenge yourself; it's the only way to get stronger. Comfort is the enemy; of great boxers, of great salespeople, of anyone who wants more, better, faster, new.

As you continue on your quest to be a champion in sales, refer back often to these **Six Ways to Consistently Challenge Yourself**. They will help you grow, learn, and earn no matter what your position:

1. **Stretch**: Avoid getting comfortable. Stretch often, stretch hard and then... stretch some more. For instance, if you're used to partnering with Andy on sales calls every week, ask to partner with someone else for a change. No offense to Andy, but getting out of your comfort zone can often help you grow.

2. **Measure**: What are your numbers? Where is your growth? Where have you been? Where are you going? Measuring progress is the surest way to see where you've been, where you need to go and how you've been doing along the way. Sales shouldn't look like a dome,

where it's high in the middle and lower at the start and the finish; there *is* no finish in sales. Make your career look like a high-rise, with each job a new floor built on the old one.

3. **Discuss**: Don't keep it all inside. Often our work is done in a vacuum, and we need to talk things out to process what we're doing right, wrong or in between. Find trusted friends, neighbors, mentors, colleagues, and family members to talk issues over with; and then listen!

4. **Question**: Even when things are going great, they could always be going better. Question every success to see not only what went right, but what went wrong. It's part of growth to always want to get better; questions help us do just that.

5. **Learn**: Always...be...learning. Take classes, read books, talk, discuss, mentor, be mentored, listen. As much as you

think you know, there is always more *to* know.

6. **Network**: Align yourself with a network full of successful people. Even if you have nothing in common with them yet, being around smart, talented, capable, and motivated people will rub off. It's true that who you associate with will ultimately affect you. Why not be affected upward, rather than downward?

# PARTING WORDS ABOUT GOING PRO: TRAINING CAMP

Changing your weight class, and changing it often, requires a strategy. You want to know when is the right time to move up, and where to go. Fortunately, there are things you can do every *day*, every *week* and every *month* to better prepare yourself for the transition from the amateur ranks to the pros; here are three of them:

- **A Jab (something new you can do today)**: *Assess the situation.* Today, spend time looking at exactly where you are. Don't cloud the issue; describe your situation realistically and face facts. Then, armed with that knowledge, make a decision. Do you want to stay where you are and achieve more, or take steps to move on and achieve more elsewhere? Either decision is fine; you just have to make it. Today!

- **A Cross (something new you can do this week)**: *Have a goal.* Once you've decided to stick around and excel to your highest potential or move on and take your sales experience to the next level, it's time to make a simple goal and stick to it. It could be to get a promotion in your current company, take a class to prepare yourself for a promotion, go back to school, increase your sales quota by 25 percent, or dust off your resume for that next sales opportunity at another company. This week is all about setting a specific goal that you know you can reach.

- **An Uppercut (something new you can do this month)**: *Reach it.* Now you have thirty days to reach that goal. This could mean updating your resume, going on interviews, or getting callbacks. It could mean staying put and getting that promotion to put you in a better position to move on to the next company when you're ready. Either way, take the next thirty days to reach the goal you've set for yourself.

# ROUND 7:
# OUT OF THE DRESSING ROOM,
## *Or:Professional Dress*

In sales, it's important that you don't leave anything to chance; not even your wardrobe. I know that professional dress can seem like just another kind of "soft" skill, but...who cares? Seriously, skill is skill—soft or hard. Any advantage you can have in the sales game counts.

How you dress is no different:

# THE POWER OF THE PANTS: HOW FASHION MATTERS

Image is everything.

You can argue with that statement all you want, but many a fight has been won before the other boxer has even stepped in the ring. A badass robe, the song a boxer chooses on his way into the ring, even the colors of his shorts—to say nothing of how cut or ripped or physically imposing he is—has serious emotional and even physical effects on his opponent.

And if your mind is already beaten, your body will surely follow.

Face it: we all know folks who just straight-up look like they have their shit together. No matter how together we think we are, the cut of their suit, their shoes, their watch, their hair, even though there's not a price tag dangling, you just know they have to be doing better than you are.

Are they really? Or have they simply tapped into what I call "the power of the pants"? Basically, the power of the pants states that fashion matters; that how you look does have an unconscious affect on how people rate you.

And it's all about the ratings.

When you walk in the room, in five seconds or less, people rate you; they categorize, label, and sequester you out into a certain "place" in their mind. It's not a sophisticated system, but it's highly powerful. In short, you are either *someone who matters* or *someone who doesn't.*

People buy from folks who matter; they ignore people who don't.

Is it right? No.

Is it politically correct? Not even close.

Does how you dress have anything to do with your intelligence, skill, expertise, or experience? *Hell* no.

Do people do this every single day? Hell *yes!*

You are in a highly competitive world where appearance counts. Your company has hired you to represent it to the world. You have to be able to go toe-to-toe with people who make more than you, have more schooling than you, are older, younger, wiser, tougher, or smarter than you; how you dress is a big factor in pulling that off.

Don't believe me? Try selling something, anything, to Donald Trump while wearing a tie with a stain on it. Or baggy pants or a skirt that's too short. The man notices everything and, right or wrong, will likely toss you out of his office for far less!

And you know what? I don't blame him. If you can't take the time to dress well for a very important meeting with an even more important client (and they're *all* important), what else are you ignoring in your life?

Face it; how you dress says a lot about you. Now we just have to find out what it's saying— and how loud.

# PROFESSIONAL DRESS IS PART OF BEING PROFESSIONAL: SIX TIPS FOR LOOKING YOUR BEST

Clearly, *how you dress* is a critical part of making a good first impression. You simply have to dress professionally to enter the professional sales arena; no ifs, ands, or buts. I'm with Donald Trump—I can't stand seeing a sloppy or cheaply dressed salesperson; it's a personal and professional affront to me as someone who takes my craft seriously.

And no, it doesn't have to cost a ton of money to dress well. Here are some simple steps you can use every day to look your best:

# STEP 1: ASSESS

The first step to dressing well is to see where you stand right now. Do you have a reputation as a good dresser? Did you get "best dressed" in high school? I went to school with a guy who wore a suit every Friday. In high school! He never got razzed or teased about it because, frankly, the guy looked good in those suits and they were good suits. Point is, I'm pretty sure he's still a natty dresser—and damn proud of it.

Or...have you never really cared about clothes? Do you just throw what's clean on and figure you'll overpower your dull, drab, or non-existent fashion sense with your "take no prisoners" sales skills? The fact is, people are watching; and not just those you're selling to, but those you're selling *with*.

Promotions, bonuses, good sales partners, better sales routes, the best accounts, the hot new products, these are all on the line every day at work, and while a horrible salesperson will never get them just because he or she dresses well, even the best salesperson might not get them if he can't even be sent out of the office because he looks like a hobo.

So take time now to face facts. If you're a good dresser, get better. If you're a poor dresser or have never thought twice about what you put on, start thinking about it. Look through your closet and see if you have a nice variety of traditional colors, such as navy, gray, black, beige, and brown. Or do you even use a closet? Do you just wear the same thing every other day or so, rotating the same tired blue suit with the gray, or gray with the black?

Traditional colors are great, but can you do something to dress them up a bit, say with a different tie or the pink shirt instead of the same old powder blue? These are big issues we'll get to in this chapter, but for now it's critical that you take this first step and at least assess the type of dresser you are *and* the type of wardrobe you have.

Remember, knowledge is power because once you know better, you can do better.

# STEP 2: PARSE

It's human nature to reach for the baggiest, the easiest, the most comfortable, the oldest, the most familiar thing in our closets and rush out a door. But what's most comfortable or familiar isn't always what's most stylish. And if your big sales meeting just happens to be on a day when you're wearing your most comfortable, least stylish outfit, your first impression could be your only one!

To avoid this temptation, go through your closet immediately and get rid of anything that:

- Is too tight, too baggy, hugs here, or pinches there

- Is shopworn or ragged

- Is out of style

- Is too loud or, alternately, too drab

- Is stained or faded

- Is frayed or worn

I'm serious about this. Go and do it now if you're the procrastinating type who will forget by the time you finish this chapter. Whenever you do it, do it. If it's in your closet and shopworn, baggy, or stained, and you're in a rush... you'll wear it.

If it's not there, you won't.

As simple as that.

# STEP 3: SHOP

You have to have good clothes—period. I didn't say expensive clothes, but good clothes. You need to treat shopping like you do downloading the latest software for your laptop or app for your phone; clothes are *that* important.

If you're not on the upswing when it comes to money yet, or you're just starting out and can't afford to rush right out and buy five power suits at the same time, it's okay; just be aware that clothes, like software or cell phones, need to be upgraded regularly. Here are a few simple, quick, and affordable things you can do to shop regularly, but not extravagantly:

- **Buy on time**: If you see a unique suit but can't afford it with cash and your credit card's maxed out, apply for a store credit card or ask for payment plan options.

- **Join**: Join a store's email alerts or sign up to get sales flyers and coupons to stay aware of new arrivals without haunting the store personally. Many stores also offer shopper's clubs where you get a card and discounts for buying frequently or a certain amount.

- **Have personal shoppers**: If you're too busy turning the sales world on fire to stop and shop every weekend, get some help! Ask your mom, spouse, or BFF to be on the lookout for your style in your sizes. It's a awesome way to have multiple pairs of eyes on your wardrobe collection, and yet not have to physically go shopping yourself.

- **Shop online**: If you know your size and trust certain stores or brands, shop online. This is something you can do while traveling, between meetings, or on your lunch break and, I have to confess, that once you start, it can be pretty addictive!

# STEP 4: STYLE: MAKE IT PERSONAL

Each of us has our own personal style. That's the thing about style: it *is* personal. What works for your sales partner, your colleague, your Dad, your brother, or your best friend from college might not work for you. Likewise, what you see on the cover of GQ or Mademoiselle may not be the right fit for your style.

I was in the bookstore recently and saw a special collection of Malcolm Gladwell's books that included Blink and Tipping Point. The outside packaging was basically a silhouette of his signature unkempt hairstyle. Now, that's not my style, it probably isn't yours, but you have to say that professionally speaking, few people are as respect as Gladwell, so...it works for him.

What works for you? You may not be comfortable in skin-tight, fitted suits or sleek, sexy business wear for women. The thing about style is that if it's clean, if it fits, if it's well made, and looks good on you, it works. You just have to be comfortable enough in your own skin to wear it well and be confident in it.

# STEP 5: ACCESSORIZE

Shirts and skirts, pants and jackets are only the beginning of how fashion affects your sales. How you tie them together, what goes with what, and even how you accessorize what you wear plays a big part in how others perceive you. Here are some simple tips to ensure that you are always in style:

- **Color:** Color can help turn a blah suit or skirt into something special. Guys can add color with their ties or, for some guys (just not me) a handkerchief sticking out of their suit pocket. Ladies, do you really need a guy to tell you how to accessorize with color? The only point I will make is that less is more. Dressing professionally doesn't necessarily mean looking like a runway model; it's about fitting in—and then some. Make a good impression but don't let the sales call be *all* about the impression. Remember that the sale is the ultimate goal, not how many compliments you get on what you're wearing.

- **Jewelry:** I'm not a big jewelry guy and don't respond to those who are. But...I do tend to look at a guy's watch because I can tell right off if he cares about that kind of thing or not. A good watch says a lot about a person, man, or woman; the same way a good pair of shoes or the latest cell phone says, "I care." Do you care? What does your jewelry say about you? Like color, a little goes a long way!

- **Technology:** Don't forget how important a part technology plays in how you dress. The cell phone you use, the Netbook, laptop, what you carry it in, all makes a great impression. If you remember "Toby" from the West Wing, he always had impeccable three-piece suits to wear to work and then would stroll in with a backpack on his back! It worked...for him. That's the key to all of this: find out what works for you, don't just copy someone else's style if it doesn't make you look and feel comfortable.

# STEP 6: INVEST

The key to dressing professionally is to make it a habit. The same way you invest in GPS for your car so you're never late to a meeting or the occasional cell phone upgrade so that you have the latest tools to beat the competition, make your clothes a personal and professional investment.

Replace faded or stained shirts, update your tie collection whenever you see a sale, and recognize that a good suit is worth its weight in gold. Consider your closet another area of your life that you update every few weeks or months. When you get into the habit of dressing professionally, you'll truly capture "the power of the pants!"

# BEYOND THE CLOTHES: CLEANLINESS COUNTS!

You have to be professional to understand the power of dressing professionally. But no matter what you spend on your clothes, if you have poor personal or grooming habits, you'll still come off looking like that Pigpen character from Peanuts!

Here are some simple personal grooming tips to ensure that you're grooming yourself for more than just sales success:

- **Cleanliness counts**: Bathe every day. Shave. Use deodorant. Wash your hair, condition it, get it cut regularly. These are the basics. But you'd be surprised by how many salespeople ignore basic general hygiene issues and are surprised when no one wants to buy from them.

- **The "Fresh Maker":** Your breath: it matters! Make it nice, fresh, and appealing. If you don't have time to brush your teeth before every sales call, at least carry portable mouthwash (I like those travel size bottles from the drug store) in your laptop bag and use it in the restroom. Mints and gum are always good in a pinch, but careful you don't chew them during the meeting!

- **It's a sales meeting, not a singles club:** A few words about cologne and perfume—less is more. You want a scent that is pleasant and professional, not loud and enticing. I actually wear one scent to work and one scent to play, and I suggest you do the same!

- **Neatness counts:** Are you neat? I mean, in general, do you keep your desk neat? Your laptop bag? Your files, records, and so forth? Neatness is an often-overlooked form of personal hygiene but one I highly recommend. If you're sloppy at work, in your car, at restaurants, or in airports, there's no way that's not going to eventually carry over into your personal and professional dress. In fact, it may already have.

# PARTING WORDS ABOUT PROFESSIONAL DRESS: TRAINING CAMP

As this chapter shows, you really *do* have to dress your best to *be* your best. Here is a list of things you can do every day, every week, and every month to dress professionally:

- **A Jab (something new you can do today)**: *Look in the mirror.* For today, all I want you to do is to simply get up and look in the mirror. Even if you're not at home, even if you're on a plane, even if you're in between flights or meetings, you can still go to the restroom and simply look in the mirror. It won't take long.

What do you see? Are you happy with how you're presenting yourself, on or off the job? If so, congratulations. If not, what are you going to do about it?

- **A Cross (something new you can do this week)**: *Shop 'til You Drop.* This week, I want you to buy something new. If you can't afford a suit right now, that's fine; get a new tie. If you can't afford new jewelry, get a new scarf. Buy something professional, attractive, and stylish this week and make it a habit so that you are regularly adding to, refining, and building on a professional wardrobe you can be proud of.

- **An Uppercut (something new you can do this month)**: *Get a makeover.* This month I want you to take a leap and get professional guidance about your professional appearance. You might get a makeover at a salon, or styling tips from a friend whose fashion sense you trust, or even pay a consultant for one hour to give you a few fast and useful tips you can implement this month. Regardless, this month I'd like you to step outside your own comfort zone and work with a trusted friend, colleague, or expert to take your professional dress to the next level. Are you up for it?

# ROUND 8: UNDERSTANDING YOUR OPPONENTS,

*Or: Stop, Look, and Listen to Succeed*

At the end of the day, a boxing match comes down to two fighters alone in a ring. One will emerge the loser, the other the victor. Half of boxing is muscle; the other half is mind. The muscle part comes down to beating your opponent, plain and simple.

The brain part comes down to *outthinking your opponent*.

When you stop to think about it, sales is really no different. Whether you're a one-man team at a small start-up company or part of a vast sales region with a dozen colleagues at a Fortune 500 corporation, at the end of the day it's still about you and the prospect; either you'll sell him—or you won't.

But before you can outthink your opponent, you have to know him; that's where this next "Round" comes in:

# STOP, LOOK, AND LISTEN: THE THREE KEYS TO UNDERSTANDING YOUR OPPONENTS

Too often we prepare for an upcoming sales meeting by studying the prospect's needs, budget, infrastructure, latest order, and a myriad of other minute details that help us close the sale.

In fact, we study everything but the prospect himself.

All of this is critical to know, but a good fighter can step into the ring with an unknown opponent and still emerge victorious if he quickly gets up to speed by knowing his opponent.

Sure, he might take a few jabs to the ribs while learning the dude's a body hitter rather than going for the face, but the knowledge he gains will help him sew up the fight for good if he can properly act on it.

No matter how much research or background you do on a sales opponent, few skills are as important when coming face to face with a client/prospect than getting to know him.

Learning how to *stop*, *look*, and *listen* will help you know any opponent, at any time, to close any deal:

# STOP

The first step to knowing who you're dealing with is to stop; just...*stop*.

Stop selling, for a minute, stop laying it on so thick, stop schmoozing and just soak it all in. Faster isn't always better; more isn't always more. Go slower, talk less, and absorb more. Take in where you are, what kind of energy your opponent is giving off, how he presents himself.

Too often we miss critical pieces of information in the first thirty seconds of a meeting—facts that could really help us out, such as:

- How did he shake your hand?

- What's his enthusiasm level?

- How experienced is she?

- How familiar with the product line is he?

- Has he come prepared?

- Unprepared?

- Is he...guarded?

- Enthusiastic?

- Open?

- Honest?

It is often said that "the devil is in the details." Well, so is success in the science of selling. But how can you pay attention to the details if you're running around in a bluster? Train yourself to be calm, cool, and collected, even amidst the flurry of meeting and greeting a new client.

You'll think calmer, faster, and smarter and, as a result, spend less time running your mouth and more time getting to know who you're up against. In sales, that can make all the difference.

# LOOK

What you see in the first five to ten minutes of any sales meeting can tell you almost all you need to know to close a sale. In a fight, there are always those moments that can make or break a round; moments where, if the fighter had only been watching more closely, he could have exploited an exposed weakness to knock his opponent out.

Those moments are present in every sales negotiation. There are times when you need to rush in and be aggressive, and other times where you need to hold back and let the client speak himself into a corner. Either way, this much is true: you can't see those moments if you're not looking.

Here are some simple things to look for when trying to close a sale:

- **Facial expressions**: The human face is like a road map of emotions. Watch it closely, and you can literally see when someone is getting ready to make a decision; those moments count!

- **Body language**: Just like the body is a road map of emotion, the human body is like a barometer for change. Is she ready to pounce? Is she already putting the cap on her pen and distancing herself from the deal? What is her body saying that can help, or hurt, the negotiations?

- **Signs of tension**: Tension can signal a variety of things: time to move in, time to back off, even time to reschedule the meeting for a later date. Knowing the prospect is tense can help you solve his problem and overcome his objections and any use a variety of proven sales technique to *get to the close*.

- **Nervous habits**: What does he do when he's nervous? Fidget? Bite the end of his pencil? Fiddle with the hem of her skirt? Bite her lip? Often a prospect can seem confident of his position when, in fact, he's anything but. How will you know which is which if you're not looking for the proper signs?

- **Distress signals**: Is your prospect sending distress signals? Is he frequently checking his cell to see if he can okay a deal with his manager? Is she rustling through files trying to find some missing element of the deal? An opponent in distress is like a fighter on the ropes; move in and finish him off!

# LISTEN

Watching and listening closely will give you unrivaled tools to understand and master the science of selling. Therefore, the final step in getting to know your opponent is to listen; not just to what he's actually saying but to what is being said between the lines. Most people only listen to what people say, and take opponents at their words.

Sales is the study of language; what you say can often mean any number of things, which is why you have to listen and hear at the same time. In other words, listen to the words *and* hear what the prospect isn't telling you.

What can you be listening for in order to get to know who's sitting on the other side of the bargaining table better? Here are some simple cues to listen for:

- **Hesitance**: There is always that "tipping point" in any negotiation where the prospect could literally go either way. Many salespeople miss that because they rush, bluff, or assume; listen instead. Hesitance is usually a sign that the client is on the fence, and it's up to you to push her in the right direction!

- **Bluffing**: A prospect that bluffs is a prospect that can be sold; period. Bluffing is for amateurs, a cheap trick easily exposed by those in the know. Bluffing is a sign of inexperience, insecurity—or both.

- **Inexperience**: Appearances can be deceiving; that's why you need to listen *and* look. If you're listening closely, you can pick up on a prospect's inexperience as easily as if he had the word "Newbie" printed on his forehead. Remember, just because someone looks like a veteran doesn't mean he is; this could be his first time on this product line, in this division, going solo, or for this company. Using the right word in the wrong context, pronouncing the product name wrong, repeatedly, stumbling over his words, or stuttering can all point to signs of inexperience on his part—and a clear advantage on yours.

- **Shutting down**: Is the prospect shutting down? Closing up shop? Using words to terminate the deal, the conversation... even the meeting? How will you know if you're not paying attention?

- **Coming around**: Conversely, is the client leaving verbal or audio clues that she's receptive to the deal? Many a deal has been left on the table because a busy salesperson had already agreed to defeat while there were still lots of signs that success was just around the corner. Never close off a deal if there's a chance, however slim, that the prospect is suddenly coming around.

# PARTING WORDS ABOUT PROFESSIONAL DRESS: TRAINING CAMP

Stopping, looking, and listening are the three keys to knowing any prospect, on any deal, in a record amount of time. But how best to start stopping, looking, and listening in a hurry?

In as little as thirty days, you can build a healthy habit to last a career—or a lifetime. Here is a list of things you can do every day, every week, and every month to know your opponent better:

- **A Jab (something new you can do today)**: *Learn to PAUSE.* Today I want you to start building the stop, look, and listen habit by giving yourself a mental reminder to pause before speaking. Even if it's to your spouse, your roommate, your boss, or your coworker, pause. Getting in the habit of slowing down during those first few seconds of a conversation will help you stop, look, and listen every day, not just during a sales negotiation.

- **A Cross (something new you can do this week):** *Shadow a Good Watcher/ Listener.* Is there someone in your office who is an expert people person? Who looks and listens with a ninja's skill? Ask to shadow him or her this week, or just do it unofficially. See how she interacts with people; watch how she approaches a meeting, any meeting, even if it's just between the two of you!

- **An Uppercut (something new you can do this month):** *Start the process.* You'll never build a habit if you don't take the first step, so this month I want you to begin using the Stop, look, and listen framework in as many client negotiations as possible. I know change is hard, but you have to start somewhere. If you're still too flustered during meetings to get the look and listen part down, at least implement the stop aspect; pause before you speak, give yourself time to form an opinion before you talk just to hear your own voice or to fill an awkward silence. Stopping will lead to looking, and looking will lead to listening; you just have to begin the process. The good news is there's no time like the present!

# ROUND 9:
# WHOSE CORNER ARE YOU IN?

*Or: Transitioning from Selling to Developing (Training New People)*

There comes a time in every salesperson's career when he has to take what he knows and transfer it to the next generation of sales associates following him.

It's a point where he's sold enough of one product, or one dozen products, or one hundred products, to translate the science of selling for others. This point is what I call the "transitional phase" from selling to developing, and it's all part of the journey.

## THREE SIGNS YOU'RE IN THE TRANSITIONAL PHASE

The Transitional Phase doesn't just happen at the end of a career. In fact, if you're a good enough salesperson, it can happen often throughout your career. Think of the mentors who coached, trained, or schooled you along your path to success; they were in the Transitional Phase, be it at twenty-nine, thirty-nine, or seventy-nine.

Success knows no age limit or expiration date; it simply exists, and once your colleagues, your clients, your coworkers, your manager, your boss, even your CEO find out that you've mastered the science of selling, they will want to know your secret.

As a successful member of the sales profession, I feel you're duty bound to share it!

Sales isn't just a career or a job; it's a lifestyle, and those who seek to live it are encouraged to share it with others, particularly if they've lived it well. So, how will you know if you're in the transitional phase and ready to share your knowledge?

Here are five signs you're already there:

1. **People frequently come to you for advice**: In every company, sales department or branch, there is always that "go

to" person that every newbie, and even some veterans, seek advice from. If folks are "going to" you more and more often, you could be in the transitional phase.

2. **You are at the top of wherever you are**: If you're consistently on the leader board at work, getting the bonuses and the prime accounts, you're clearly ready to start developing in addition to selling.

3. **You're doing more consulting and less selling**: Finally, if you're already talking more than you're selling, consulting more, and going on fewer and fewer calls; you're likely already in the transitional phase.

# EMBRACING THE TRANSITIONAL PHASE

A certain satisfaction comes from knowing you're in a spot where your knowledge enhances and mobilizes the success of the entire department, division or, in some cases, the home office.

Many salespeople tell me they can't stand training others or sitting in an orientation walking newbies through the sales process; I love it! It's a opportune way not only to embrace and enhance what I do every day by putting the process into words for others, but it's also a rewarding way to ensure that those I come into contact with take sales seriously.

Think about it: if the good guys don't teach the new guys, who will? The bad guys, right? And who wants that? If you're proud of your profession, if you're happy with your lifestyle, if you're addicted to the challenge, the adrenaline, the chaos of making a deal, don't you want to share that with as many people as possible?

If you care about sales, you'll want to embrace the transitional phase in the same way you've embraced every other phase of your career—from being a newbie yourself to mastering the science of selling.

Here are some tips for doing just that:

- **Come prepared:** If you accept and recognize that a variety of folks will be approaching you during your transitional phase for help with their own development, come prepared. Have tips ready to share, get your "spiel" down and ready to share.

- **Take it seriously:** The more seriously you take the mentoring, coaching, and training of others, the more you'll not only enjoy it but actually make this a useful time for you and your trainees.

- **Give generously:** Was there someone who took an interest in you when you were just starting out? Did he make all the difference in you having the confidence to start, or continue, doing what you do so well now? Be that person for someone else; give generously of your time, your energy, and your expertise. Trust me; it *will* come back to you.

# THE IMPORTANCE OF PROPER DEVELOPMENT: THE FOUR TRAITS OF A GOOD COACH/MENTOR/TRAINER

Why is development so important?

Well, if you care about the science of selling or the profession of sales, you'll want to keep it in the hands of the most qualified, the most energetic, and the most talented salespeople, right?

The kinds of people who tend to seek out mentors, consultants, advisors, and coaches are *exactly* the type of folks you want in sales for the long haul: motivated, aggressive, ambitious, and eager to learn.

So where do *you* fit in?

Your role in development is to show them the right ways, the smart ways, the personal ways you've succeeded so that they can not only follow in your footsteps but also feel free to put their own stamp on success as well.

Transitioning from sales to training, from success to development requires a few adjustments along the way. In short, good developers, coaches, and trainers all share the same four traits:

- **Skill**: First and foremost, you must be skilled at what you do. But you must also believe in your own skill. If you keep telling newbies, "Hey, kid, I just got lucky," that's not helping anybody. Trust your skill, own it, and then share it.

- **Confidence**: Not only must you be skillful, you must be confident that you are skillful. That means not being too modest or downplaying your success. Own what you've done, know that you're now in an advisory role because the powers that be respect and admire you, and quit worrying if it's going to sound like you're bragging!

- **Patience**: It takes patience to nurture others. Even if you're a hard-ass on the sales floor, you can still be a hard-ass coach—just be a patient one. Seriously, new sales folks won't often get it the first time, so they'll come back again and again. That's okay; it's part of what you do now.

- **Authority**: Last but not least, teach like a teacher. I don't know about you, but my best teachers were authoritative. They kept the student-teacher role strictly professional and it was always one of mutual respect. You can be friendly, but those you mentor need a teacher more than they need a friend.

# PARTING WORDS ABOUT TRANSITIONING TO DEVELOPMENT: TRAINING CAMP

Transitioning into a developmental role may take time to get used to. After all, few companies will let you off the sales hook completely, and who would want to stop selling altogether simply to develop?

Here are three things you can do this day, this week, and this month to ensure that you manage both your responsibilities—sales and development—equally well:

- **A Jab (something new you can do today)**: *Prepare.* Even if you aren't formally in the developmental role yet, begin to transition into it by preparing how you might answer some of the most common sales questions. Draw up a list of five to ten questions and write down some quick answers. You may even refine these into a handout you can provide those who seek your advice—something that's easily printable or attachable via email. Always have them available so that you can refer to them when in the development mode.

- **A Cross (something new you can do this week):** *Learn from the best.* If you're uncomfortable being in the development mode, do something about it! Take time this week to sign up for a course on teaching or mentoring, even if it's via audio or DVD. Sign up for a seminar on interpersonal communication or tutoring. Don't assume that just because you can sell and negotiate you can also develop equally well, at least not without some additional development of your own!

- **An Uppercut (something new you can do this month):** *Find a guinea pig!* Take this month to find someone who's willing to be developed and fine tune your process for developing him. It could be a college student, an intern at work, or a newbie at the sales department. Offer your services and help him to understand that while this may be your first time developing someone new, you take it very seriously and want the best for him. Chances are, you'll have folks lining up around the block!

# ROUND 10:
## CROWD PLEASER(S),

*Or: Motivating Teams for Success (Creating a Positive Sales Culture)*

Have you ever heard the saying, "I'm in your corner"? Sure you have, but did you ever bother to ask yourself where it came from. The fact is it's a boxing term. As we've all seen in fight movies, the trainer, manager, or whoever feels the fighter trusts the most stands in his corner.

When someone says, "I'm in your corner," it means they're behind you, 100 percent. But it's more than just emotional support or Rocky-moment encouragement; being in someone's corner is about offering him support, advice, and even tough love when he needs it.

Now that you've transitioned from sales to development, you're in a whole lot of corners; your sales team(s), individual salespeople, even the bosses, coaches, managers, and mentors who gave you the opportunity to lead instead of sell.

Now it's your job to encourage others by creating a positive sales culture that encourages your people to learn, try new things, experiment with what might work and what might not, and generally create a sales team that masters the science of selling:

# IT'S ALL ABOUT SELLING, OR: WHY POSITIVITY MATTERS

Whenever I begin developing a new team, class, or office full of salespeople, there is always that straggler, "doom and gloomer" or just plain Negative Nancy who questions why we can't just get to selling.

The fact is, it's *all* about selling; every soft skill, hard skill, class, lecture, seminar, retreat, conference, lunch break, or employee evaluation is a learning opportunity if you're open to become better at what you're called to do.

Unfortunately, too many of the lessons you learn about selling are negative. It's hard, it's challenging, the odds suck, the product sucks, the client sucks, the moral sucks, the job sucks… the career sucks.

It's how burnout happens and poten-tially good—scratch that, *great*-salespeople burn out, fry, fizzle, or fade before they ever get a chance to shine. Is selling hard? Sure. Challenging? Every day. Do the odds and, occasionally, even the products suck? Sure, of course.

But the fact of the matter is that there are two ways to face every challenge: as *adversity* or *opportunity*. You need to get your people in the habit of seeing challenge as opportunity in order to avoid adversity.

# THREE STEPS TO A POSITIVE SALES CULTURE

How do you transition from challenge to success? What can you do to take an ordinary sales office and turn it into a self-generating positivity machine? (Okay, or at least a place where folks can actually thrive, learn, and grow?)

One way to do just that is to create, develop, and then foster a positive sales culture:

# STEP 1: CREATE

You have to build it before you can develop it. Because so many sales cultures are built on the bottom line of price, numbers, and sales reports at the cost of personal development, this may mean turning a hostile environment into a positive one.

Start with yourself. Are you a positive developer? Do you encourage, nurture, and support or simply harangue, yell, and pretend to care? Don't get me wrong; I'm not suggesting that you turn the sales office into a "peace, love, and kittens" place to work, but you do have to recognize that hostility is a dead end and leads only to adversity.

Once you've come to a place where you recognize and value positivity as an effective teaching tool, begin leading by example. Praise not just the noteworthy accomplishments but also the minor ones as well. Be vocal about it; get in the habit of saying something positive to every member of your sales team, every day.

Encourage them to do the same.

# STEP 2: DEVELOP

Creating a positive sales culture is one thing; developing it is quite the other. It's human nature to get all excited about something, get started, and then...let it ride into the sunset without ever doing much to develop or foster its growth.

Well, a positive sales culture isn't like a cactus; you can't just plant the idea and walk away and expect it to grow anyway. Instead, it's more like a rose bush; it needs to be watered, fed, nourished, and developed into something you can be proud of.

Here are several tips for developing the positive sales culture you've just created:

- **Have a plan**: In order to develop a positive sales culture you need to make it routine, regular, and consistent. It's no good encouraging your sales team one day and then haranguing them the next. Make a plan that includes what you plan to do to make your office a more positive one; then stick to it.

- **Set a schedule**: Habits are formed when you follow a routine. Look at the calendar this month and schedule what you need to do, and when, and even where, and particularly how often according to your plan above.

- **Make a list**: As part of that plan/schedule, make a list of the several things you plan to do daily, weekly, and monthly to increase positivity in the sales office. This could include a daily round table discussion designed to encourage effective sales tactics, a daily word of positivity, or a breakfast meeting every Thursday. Whatever it is, commit to it by putting it in your weekly calendar and making it consistent. Telling the group you'll be doing this "every week from now on" and then skipping the next three weeks is no way to build a habit; or positivity.

- **Check it twice**: Positivity needs reinforcement to grow. Develop your positive sales culture by doubling up on the positive things you do. For instance, don't just meet with your people once a week; meet with them twice a week. Don't just offer one kind word per person per day, offer two. The more you generate positivity from within, the more your people will embody it without.

# STEP 3: FOSTER

Fostering a positive sales culture is all about the long haul. It's not about today or even tomorrow, but next week, next month, and next year. It's not just about this new hire, but the person that new hire trains next year. It's about leading by example to create positive people who will reflect back on you, the product, and eventually the company.

In short, fostering is about the future. In order to foster a more positive future for your entire department, enlist the entire department's help:

- Create a buddy system where new hires are placed with veteran salespeople.

- Have a suggestion box for ways to be more positive, more often.

- Have a system in place for training new people right the first time.

- Enlist as many senior people in your positivity plan as possible.

# PARTING WORDS ABOUT CREATING A POSITIVE SALES CULTURE: TRAINING CAMP

As we have seen, creating a positive sales culture requires a co-commitment from you *and* your sales team. Oftentimes encouraging your team can be as challenging as selling a product or service to another client or business.

Here are some things you can do this day, this week, and this month to ensure that your sales culture is the most positive one possible:

- **A Jab (something new you can do today)**: *Enlist.* Find a point person to help you. Today, right now, identify a colleague, assistant, mentor, or coach to help you rally the troops even when you're not around. Two heads are always better than one, and never more so than when trying to encourage an often discouraged sales team.

- **A Cross (something new you can do this week)**: *Celebrate success.* Positivity never comes from negativity; this much is true. You have to breed positivity with more positivity, so this week spend time celebrating the good in every one of your people. Schedule a time to visit with each one this week, and treat "super sellers" to extra special rewards like taking them to lunch or dinner or other perks you know they'll enjoy (within reason). I'm not saying to cheer on failure or celebrate those who contribute nothing, but if they're on your sales team in the first place chances are they must bring something to the table; focus on what, exactly, that is this week.

- **An Uppercut (something new you can do this month)**: *Work toward a goal.* Use the next thirty days to work toward a specific goal; it doesn't even have to be a certain sales figure—or, if it is, a significantly higher one. Pick a goal you know the sales team can achieve, like a small 5-percent bump in sales or a dollar figure you're reasonably comfortable they can achieve. The goal at this point isn't so much the results you're seeking but the team effort and positivity that goes into reaching that goal together.

# ROUND 11:
## STAYING A CHAMPION,
*Or: Succession Planning (Exit strategy)*

If you've ever had the misfortune to watch an aging fighter endure a punishing last fight, then you've seen a boxer with no exit strategy. And who can blame him? Few fighters ever imagine the ends of their careers the first time they bound into the ring, and yet the most successful fighters aren't those who stay in the longest, but those who have a plan for leaving the game when the time is right for them.

Mastering the science of selling also requires a clear vision of not just the beginning of your career, but the final phase as well. That's why I've been hitting so hard on development these last few chapters; phasing from straight-up sales to developing sales leaders is just the beginning of something called *succession planning*.

# WHAT IS SUCCESSION PLANNING?

The idea at the heart of succession planning revolves around one basic question: Who will your successor(s) be? In other words, who will follow in your footsteps? Who will you train to take your place? Who will you pass the baton to? Or, in boxing terms, who will wear your gloves after you've slipped from the ring for the very last time?

As one might imagine, choosing a successor is no easy feat. It requires careful planning, attention to detail and people skills. That's why the last few chapters on developing talent and creating a positive sales environment were so well timed; you're in a great spot to handpick your successor from your current talent pool!

# FIVE SIGNS OF A WORTHY SUCCESSOR

Key to successful succession planning is finding the right successor. You don't want someone exactly like you but, instead, someone who has their own style of leadership and sales expertise who can master the science of selling in his own unique way.

While your own personal "must-haves" will vary for each position and every candidate, here are five signs that you should be looking for in any worthy successor:

1. **Punctuality**: Time is critical in sales, and someone who can't be trusted to show up on time is, frankly, someone who can't be trusted as a worthy successor. While we all have emergencies that make us late occasionally, chronic lateness is simply a sign of disrespect. So watch for a pattern of punctuality to prove that someone is really worthy to take your place.

2. **Attention to detail**: Every deal I've ever done has always come down to the details; giving an inch here to gain a foot there. But you have to know which details matter, and which don't, in order to make those kinds of judgment calls.

3. **People skills**: Sales is about people, bottom line. If your successor has good sales despite his people skills, it's usually a run of good luck that's not likely to last.

4. **Drive**: Every sales leader I've ever met has been driven to achieve amazing things in the world of sales. They truly understand and master the science of selling.

5. **Empathy**: Finally, look for someone who does more than just sell but who cares. Who cares about his coworkers, his assistant, his boss, and his clients. Not only is empathy a human quality we all need to live, but it's a critical sales skill when trying to solve a client's problem.

## HOW TO STAY A CHAMPION: FIVE STEPS TO SUCCESSION PLANNING

You've seen what to look for in a worthy successor, now you need the tools necessary to put him in your place. Here are five simple steps to succession planning that will help you put the right person into the right position at the right time:

1. **Be on the lookout:** You can't find the right person if you aren't even looking. The time to start choosing your rightful successor isn't the day before you retire but weeks, months, even years in advance.

2. **Create a checklist:** You should have an internal or actual list of qualities and skills you're looking for in a worthy successor, such as punctuality, people skills, attention to detail, strong sales numbers, and willingness to learn. Establish a set number of qualities your successor must have to qualify, and check off each quality for each potential successor.

3. **Narrow your choices down:** You need to be actively whittling down your potential successor list with regularity. If you start with a dozen potential candidates on

May first and you plan on leaving June eighth, you need to regularly take one or two people off your list to get down to your final two to three choices. It will be much easier to choose between two or three people than, say, twelve or thirteen.

4. **Play devil's advocate:** Oftentimes you might find someone who looks good on paper, but crumbles under pressure, or is a horrible leader and wouldn't spend a moment cultivating the positive sales culture you worked so hard to build. Don't be afraid to test your successor from time to time to see if he will truly nurture the strong sales legacy you hope to leave behind.

5. **Build a relationship:** Finally, a strong succession plan is built on an even stronger relationship. Take time to nurture your successor much as you nurtured the sales department you're leaving behind.

# PARTING WORDS ABOUT FINDING YOUR SUCCESSOR: TRAINING CAMP

The next day, week, and month can find you much closer to finding a worthy successor if you make time for the fooling jabs, crosses and uppercuts to ensure that you find the right person to fill the hole you're leaving behind:

- **A Jab (something new you can do today)**: *Build your successor list.* Right now, today, start with a blank piece of paper and brainstorm anyone and everyone who might be the right fit for your job. Don't worry if the list starts with everyone in your sales department; you will be using the following week(s) and month to whittle it down carefully.

- **A Cross (something new you can do this week)**: *Narrow down your choices.* Once you've compiled your master list of potential replacements, use this week to begin narrowing it down. Some people won't want your job, others won't be able to handle the pressure, and some will want it too badly, so you'll probably find it easier than you think to pare the list down into a manageable size.

- **An Uppercut (something new you can do this month):** *Identify your top-five candidates.* Even if you're not leaving for a year, you need a manageable list— and plenty of time—to find a successor who's worthy enough to fill your shoes. So by the end of this month you should have a list of your top-five candidates. This will give you the time to meet with each one individually, perhaps repeatedly, to ensure that you have the time, energy, and opportunity to find just the right person.

# ROUND 12:
# THROWING IN THE TOWEL,
## *Or: Knowing When to Retire*

Every fighter faces the reality one day: it's time to throw in the towel. Some don't face it soon enough, and wind up sticking around a little too long. Others throw in the towel too soon, and miss out on the career satisfaction of leaving on an all-time high.

The key is to not retire too soon or too late, but instead to make positive choices about when it's the right time for you to begin transitioning from succeeding in sales to succeeding after sales:

# WHY IT'S OKAY TO THROW IN THE TOWEL

The good news about retirement is that, these days, it's not about quitting, it's about transitioning. I know lots of retired people; very few of them are inactive. Oftentimes the most success retirees are also the most successful consultants, coaches, mentors, and trainers—whether they're getting paid for it or not.

The key is to begin thinking about retirement well before you set an actual timeline for your departure from your present company or sales altogether. Why am I talking about retirement in the same breath as I talk about mastering the science of selling?

Precisely because mastery is about preparation; being prepared for the future—even if it's twenty years down the line—helps you plan for it so that there are no surprises when that day actually arises.

Don't consider retirement a failure, or even an ending to your successful sales story. Instead, consider it a transition to a place where you can use your decades of sales expertise in a way that fits with your present lifestyle.

After all, you could be merely transitioning from sales to development, development to freelance consultant, or merging to be VP of a new company specializing in sales. You could teach, consult, coach, mentor, or even...write a book about sales!

# SIX SIGNS IT MIGHT BE TIME TO THROW IN THE TOWEL

When will you know the right time to throw in the towel? While the actual causes for retirement/transition differ for every sales leader, here are six standard signs that mean it might be time for you to throw in the towel:

1. **You're at a success plateau**: In my office we have a saying: "Salespeople are used to high and lows, but never plateaus!" If you've been flat-lined too long, it could be time for you to put your energy and enthusiasm elsewhere.

2. **You're already eyeing your replacement**: If you find yourself looking around the office thinking, "He'd be a great

replacement," chances are you're not planning on sticking around too long!

3. **Your heart lies elsewhere**: It could be at another company, in another industry, in your own entrepreneurial endeavor, or simply on a yacht someplace, but when your heart's no longer in sales, it's time to go.

4. **You feel your enthusiasm waning**: As we all know, enthusiasm is the fuel on which a successful sales career runs. If you find it harder and harder to fill that tank, it might be time to go.

5. **Your performance has peaked:** Are your highest numbers behind you? Has it been awhile since you've found yourself on the leader board at work? Oftentimes performance suffers when we're not performing at our peak levels. And oftentimes we're not performing at our peak levels because we've already mentally "checked out" from the job.

6. **You're more interested in getting out than going in**: I've always said that, like boxing, sales isn't a job (or a sport) so much as a lifestyle. We can give twelve hours a day and still have more when we're on fire for the job and proud of our accomplishments and "in that mode." But when it's time to go, we often find ourselves spending less and less time on actual selling, and more and more time on, well...anything else!

# PARTING WORDS ABOUT THROWING IN THE TOWEL: TRAINING CAMP

When it comes right down to it, throwing in the towel isn't quite so easy as, well, simply throwing in the towel. There are timelines to consider, and not just yours but those of all your accounts, for instance, and the successor you've chosen as part of your succession plan.

To make sure that you leave your position appropriately, thoroughly, and without burning any bridges behind you, take time to focus on today, this week, and this month as you finalize your terms of employment:

- **A Jab (something new you can do today)**: *Make your intentions known.* You might think the whole office knows about your imminent departure, but the fact is that there is a way to go about leaving a position properly. Start at the top, with your boss, and ask him who else could or should need to know—and when. Tell those who need to know now, and use good judgment to tell the rest at an appropriate time.

- **A Cross (something new you can do this week)**: *Identify your successor.* Now that you've formerly announced your retirement, it's time to make a formal decision about your successor. Not only do you know who's going to be taking your place, but so does that person.

- **An Uppercut (something new you can do this month):** *Begin a smooth transition.* Once you've made your intentions known and identified your successor, you can gradually begin the transition process by switching out your files and bringing him around to meet your clients (if you haven't already done so). This might take more than month, but typically, it takes at least a month.

# ABOUT THE AUTHOR:

*Dave Saben*

Dave brings over 12 years' experience as a professional sales leader with an expertise that spans a full range of industries from technology to e-learning. Dave specializes in the development of sales educational methodologies that appeal to all audiences.. Dave started his career in telecommunications where he held several titles from National Account Manager to Regional Vice President. For the last 4 years Dave was employed by Ascend Learning a premier provider of educational materials to colleges and universities. He served as Director of National Accounts. In this role Mr. Saben single handedly increased market penetration by 400% in under 9 months.

After his tenure as a Director of National Accounts, Dave was Vice President of Sales for the National Healthcareer Association (a subsidiary of Acsend Learning), the nation's largest provider of healthcare certifications. Under

Dave's leadership he hired and developed a high octane sales group that doubled NHA revenue in less than 12 months.

In his free time he and his wife Margy run a nonprofit athletic club www.tinytotsportsclub.org. The club is for young children, ages 3 – 5, where they learn the value of sportsmanship and teamwork. They run classes in tee-ball, soccer and football. Dave is a graduate from the University of Miami where he majored in business management with a minor in entre-preneurism. Dave and Margy live in West Palm Beach, FL with their son Dylan,daughter Anabella and two dogs